FUN FA
FOR GO

© 2009 by Barbour Publishing, Inc.

ISBN 978-1-60260-374-5

Scripture quotations marked NIV are taken from the HOLY BIBLE, NEW INTERNATIONAL VERSION®. NIV®. Copyright © 1973, 1978, 1984 by International Bible Society. Used by permission of Zondervan. All rights reserved.

Scripture quotations marked KJV are taken from the King James Version of the Bible.

Scripture quotations marked J. B. PHILLIPS are taken from *The New Testament in Modern English*, published by HarperCollins.

Published by Barbour Publishing, Inc., P.O. Box 719, Uhrichsville, Ohio 44683, www.barbourbooks.com

Our mission is to publish and distribute inspirational products offering exceptional value and biblical encouragement to the masses.

Printed in the United States of America.

FUN FACTS
FOR GOLFERS

BARBOUR
PUBLISHING

The History of Golf

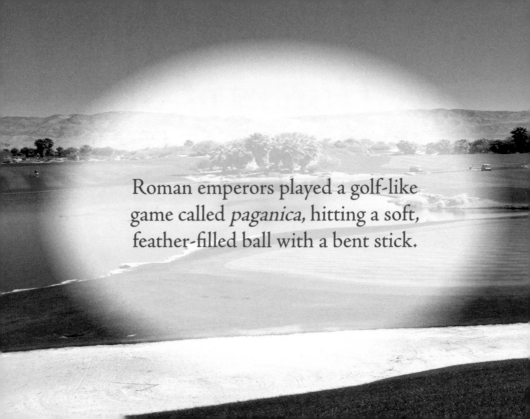

Roman emperors played a golf-like game called *paganica*, hitting a soft, feather-filled ball with a bent stick.

A Dutch game resembling golf—
het kolven—was played in the
American colonies in the 1650s.

Other golf-like games were
played by the Belgians (*chole*),
the French (*jeu de mail*),
and the Italians (pall mall).

Author J. R. R. Tolkien describes the invention of golf in his novel *The Hobbit*:

[The hobbit Bullroarer] charged the ranks of the goblins of Mount Gram in the Battle of The Green Fields, and knocked their king Golfimbul's head clean off with a wooden club. It sailed a hundred yards through the air and went down a rabbit hole, and in this way the battle was won, and the game of Golf invented at the same moment.

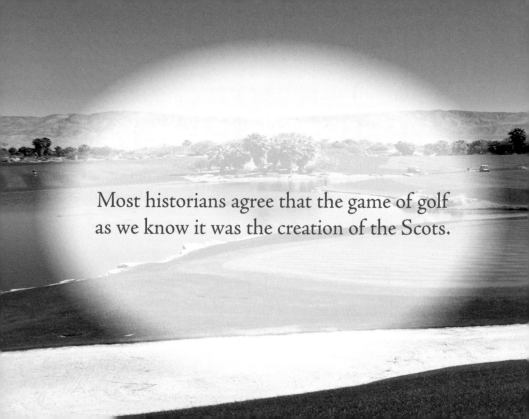

Most historians agree that the game of golf
as we know it was the creation of the Scots.

In the beginning God created
the heavens and the earth.

GENESIS 1:1 NIV

The name *golf* apparently derives from the medieval Dutch *kolf,* meaning "club."

The word golf is not an acronym for "gentlemen only, ladies forbidden."

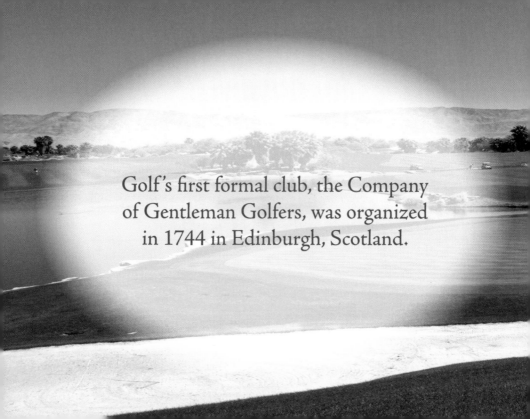

Golf's first formal club, the Company of Gentleman Golfers, was organized in 1744 in Edinburgh, Scotland.

The St. Andrews Ladies' Golf Club
was founded in 1867.

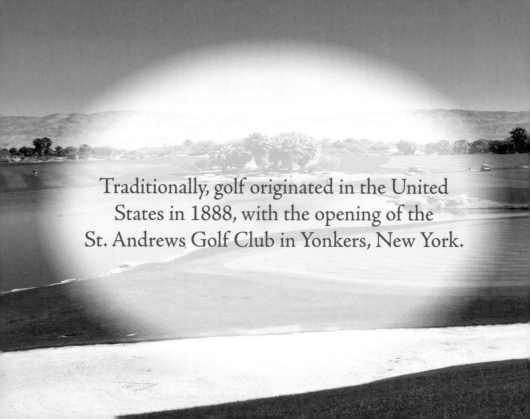

Traditionally, golf originated in the United States in 1888, with the opening of the St. Andrews Golf Club in Yonkers, New York.

But historians say a shipment of 96 clubs and 432 balls from Scotland was received at Charleston, South Carolina, in 1743.

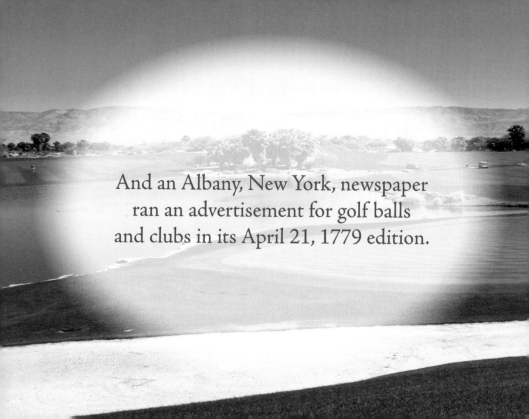

And an Albany, New York, newspaper
ran an advertisement for golf balls
and clubs in its April 21, 1779 edition.

Golf Equipment

United States Golf Association–approved golf balls must weigh no more than 1.62 ounces.

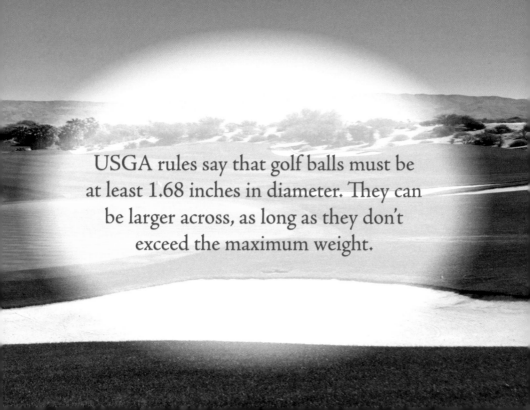

USGA rules say that golf balls must be at least 1.68 inches in diameter. They can be larger across, as long as they don't exceed the maximum weight.

Most golf balls have between 330 and 500 dimples.

"Even the very hairs of your
head are all numbered."

Matthew 10:30 niv

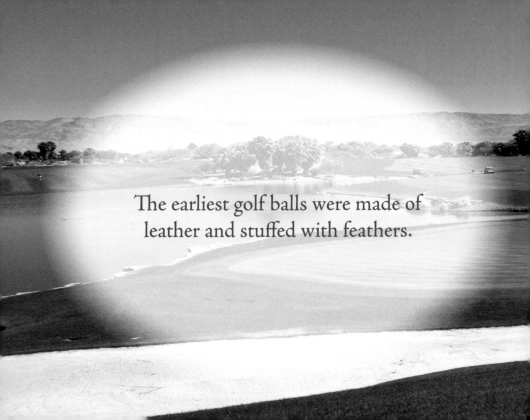

The earliest golf balls were made of leather and stuffed with feathers.

Other early golf balls were leather sacks stuffed with cow hair or were carved from wood.

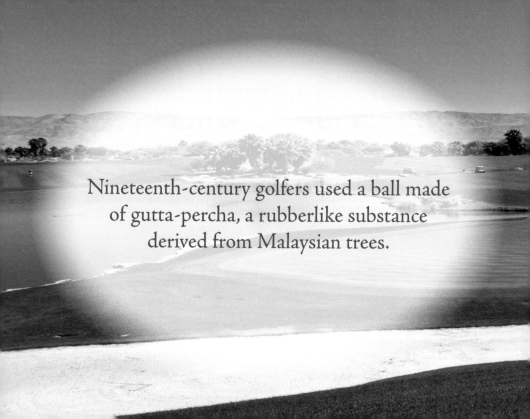

Nineteenth-century golfers used a ball made of gutta-percha, a rubberlike substance derived from Malaysian trees.

The cheaper, mass-produced gutta-percha balls are credited with the rapid spread of golf in the nineteenth century.

"Gutties" were either rolled
by hand or formed in a mold.

Don't let the world around you squeeze you into its own mould, but let God re-mould your minds from within.

ROMANS 12:2 J. B. PHILLIPS

Early golf balls were smooth; nineteenth-century advancements brought pebbling, gridlike cross-hatching, and rifled grooves.

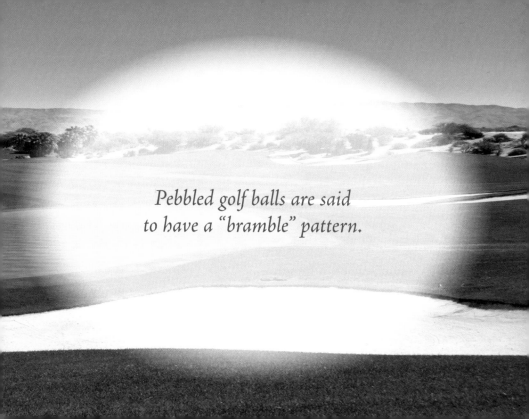

Pebbled golf balls are said
to have a "bramble" pattern.

A 1920s golf ball manufactured by Faroid featured a pattern of raised concentric rings and the stamped message THIS END UP.

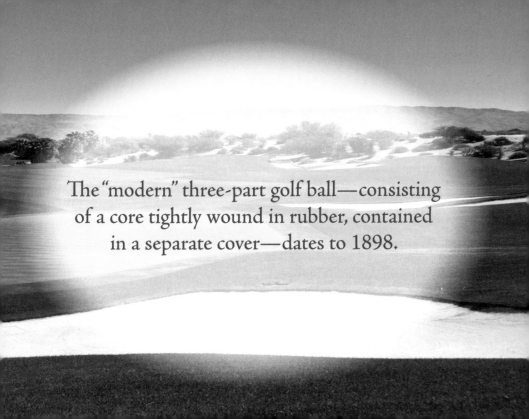

The "modern" three-part golf ball—consisting
of a core tightly wound in rubber, contained
in a separate cover—dates to 1898.

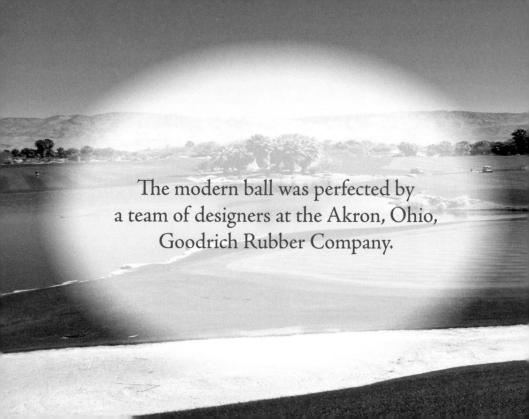

The modern ball was perfected by
a team of designers at the Akron, Ohio,
Goodrich Rubber Company.

A "sand mold," patented in 1895, helped golfers form teelike mounds from handfuls of sand.

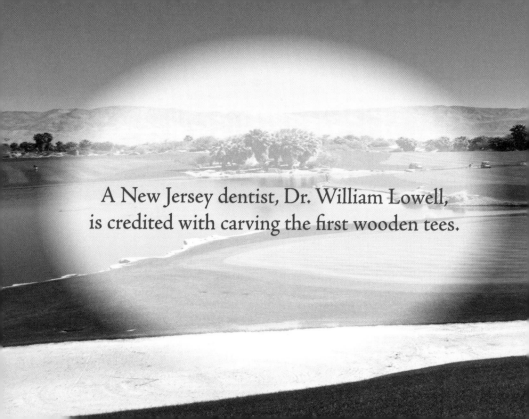

A New Jersey dentist, Dr. William Lowell,
is credited with carving the first wooden tees.

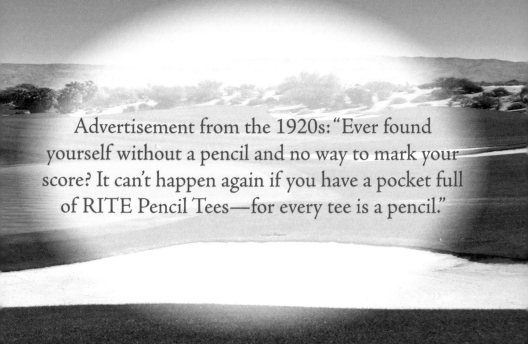

Advertisement from the 1920s: "Ever found yourself without a pencil and no way to mark your score? It can't happen again if you have a pocket full of RITE Pencil Tees—for every tee is a pencil."

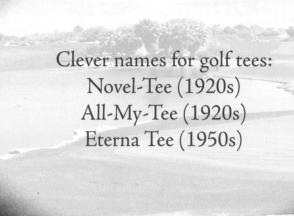

Clever names for golf tees:
Novel-Tee (1920s)
All-My-Tee (1920s)
Eterna Tee (1950s)

O Lord God Almighty, who is like you?

Psalm 89:8 niv

Early wooden club shafts were made of hazel, ash, and then hickory.

Primitive golf clubs had long "noses" similar to modern hockey sticks.

Steel-shaft clubs were approved
by the USGA in 1925.

The graphite shaft appeared
in the 1970s and gained popularity
on drivers in the mid-1980s.

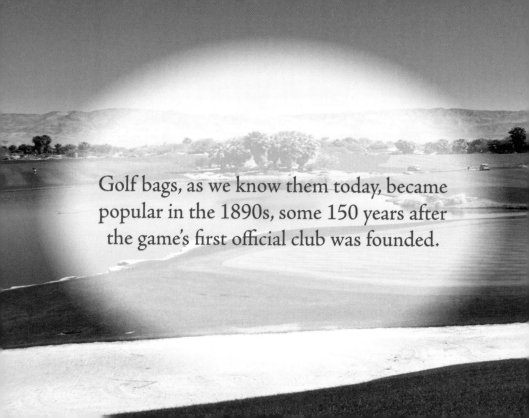

Golf bags, as we know them today, became popular in the 1890s, some 150 years after the game's first official club was founded.

Golf Courses

Early golf courses earned the name "links"
from their location on the Scottish coastline,
"linking" arable land with the sea.

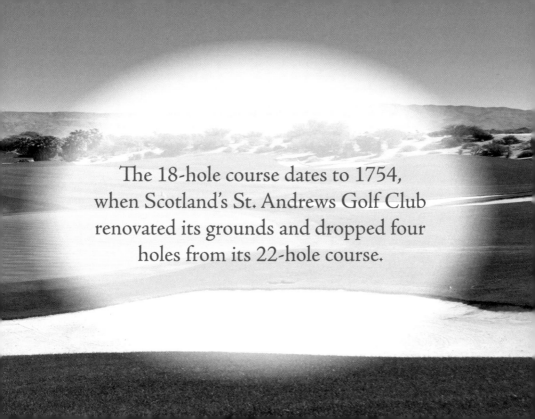

The 18-hole course dates to 1754,
when Scotland's St. Andrews Golf Club
renovated its grounds and dropped four
holes from its 22-hole course.

The oldest golf club outside the British Isles is the Royal Calcutta in India.

The United States' oldest public golf course—built for the general population—is New York City's Van Cortlandt Golf Course. Opened in 1895, it still operates as part of the New York City parks department.

The Emirates Golf Club, in the Persian Gulf city of Dubai, is maintained in the desert with some 750,000 gallons of water each day.

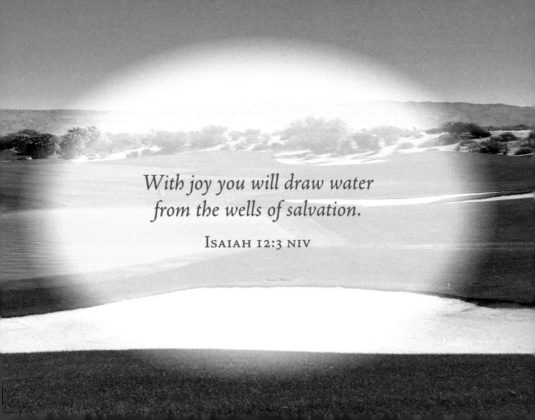

*With joy you will draw water
from the wells of salvation.*

ISAIAH 12:3 NIV

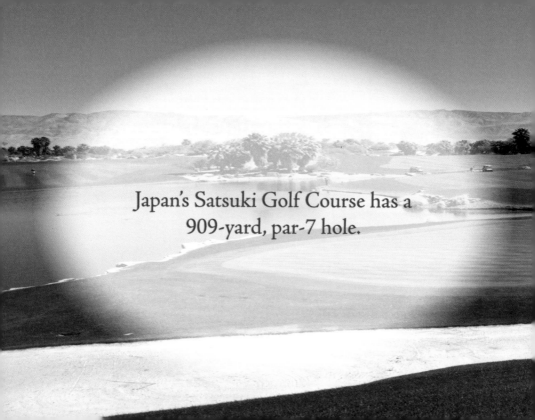

Japan's Satsuki Golf Course has a 909-yard, par-7 hole.

Michigan's Chocolay Downs course boasts a 1,007-yard par-6.

A man named Floyd Satterly Rood golfed his way from the United States' Pacific to Atlantic coasts between September 14 and October 3, 1964.

Rood recorded nearly 115,000 strokes and lost more than 3,500 balls on the 3,400-mile course.

U.S. astronaut Alan Shepard Jr., the first American in space, is also the first (and only) person to golf on the moon.

Shepard, commander of the *Apollo 14* moon landing, hit two balls on the lunar surface with a six-iron head attached to a soil sampler.

Cool names for golf holes:
Devil's Cauldron (8th hole,
Banff Springs, Alberta, Canada)
Eden (17th hole, Shinnecock Hills,
Southampton, New York)
Woe-Be-Tide (4th hole,
Turnberry, Scotland)

A good name is more desirable than great riches; to be esteemed is better than silver or gold.

PROVERBS 22:1 NIV

New Jersey's Pine Valley Golf Course boasts the world's largest sand trap—dubbed "Hell's Half Acre."

The Portal Golf Club features a hole that tees off in Saskatchewan, Canada, and ends in North Dakota—125 yards later.

Golf Magazine's
Top 18 Holes of the World (Part 1):
1. Hole #4, Banff Springs Golf Course,
Alberta, Canada
2. Hole #15, Cypress Point Club,
Pebble Beach, California
3. Hole #4, National Golf Links of America,
Southampton, New York

Golf Magazine's
Top 18 Holes of the World (Part 2):
4. Hole #17, Tournament Players Club at Sawgrass,
Ponte Vedra Beach, Florida
5. Hole #11, Old Ballybunion Golf Club,
County Kerry, Ireland
6. Hole #5, Bethpage State Park Golf Club (Black),
Farmingdale, New York

Golf Magazine's
Top 18 Holes of the World (Part 3):
7. Hole #16, Merion Golf Club (East),
Ardmore, Pennsylvania
8. Hole #5, Mid Ocean Club,
Tucker's Town, Bermuda
9. Hole #13, Pine Valley Golf Club,
Clementon, New Jersey

Golf Magazine's
Top 18 Holes of the World (Part 4):
10. Hole #9, Royal County Down Golf Club,
Newcastle, Northern Ireland
11. Hole #6, Royal Melbourne Golf Club (West),
Black Rock, Australia
12. Hole #17, St. Andrews Golf Club (Old),
St. Andrews, Scotland

Golf Magazine's
Top 18 Holes of the World (Part 5):
13. Hole #14, Shinnecock Hills Golf Club,
Southampton, New York
14. Hole #12, Southern Hills Golf Club,
Tulsa, Oklahoma
15. Hole #13, Augusta National Golf Club,
Augusta, Georgia

Golf Magazine's
Top 18 Holes of the World (Part 6):
16. Hole #6, Carnoustie Golf Links
(Championship), Carnoustie, Scotland
17. Hole #3, Durban Country Club,
Durban, South Africa
18. Hole #18, Pebble Beach Golf Links,
Pebble Beach, California

The Lord is my shepherd. . . .
He makes me lie down in green pastures,
he leads me beside quiet waters.

PSALM 23:1–2 NIV

The Terminology
of Golf

Birdie—
A score of one under par on a particular hole.
Possibly from a nineteenth-century slang term,
bird, meaning "very good."

Eagle—
A score of two under par on a particular hole.
Better than an everyday bird.

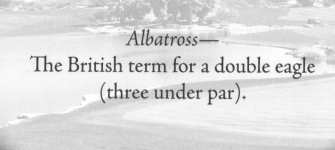

Albatross—
The British term for a double eagle
(three under par).

Rabbit—
A poor or novice player.

Rat—

What bit golfer John Morgan while he was searching for his ball in the rough of the 1968 British Open.

Thrown by the incident at Carnoustie, Scotland, Morgan scored 92 for the round.

Bogey—
A score of one over par for a particular hole.
Possibly from a line in a nineteenth-century
British song, "I'm the Bogey Man,
catch me if you can!"

The warning cry "Fore!" is said to be an abbreviation of a sixteenth-century military command, "Beware before!"

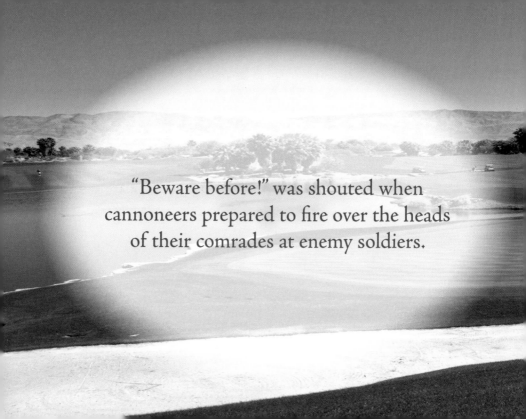

"Beware before!" was shouted when cannoneers prepared to fire over the heads of their comrades at enemy soldiers.

Beware lest ye also, being led away
with the error of the wicked,
fall from your own stedfastness.

2 PETER 3:17 KJV

The putting green has been nicknamed golf's "dance floor."

The fringe, the close-cut grass surrounding the green, is also called the "collar," the "apron," or the "frog hair."

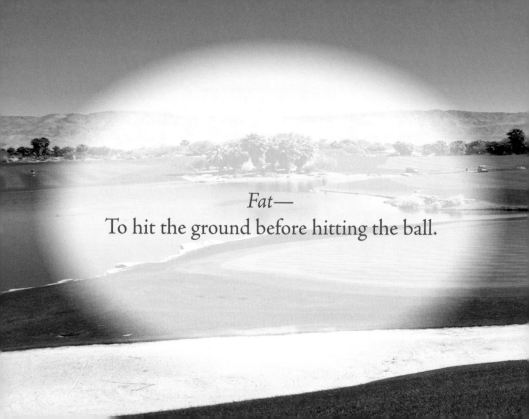

Fat—
To hit the ground before hitting the ball.

Rules and Associations

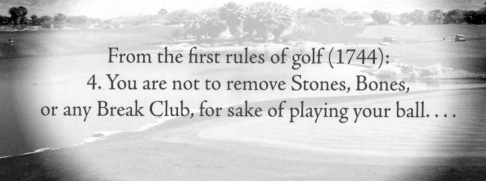

From the first rules of golf (1744):
4. You are not to remove Stones, Bones,
or any Break Club, for sake of playing your ball. . . .

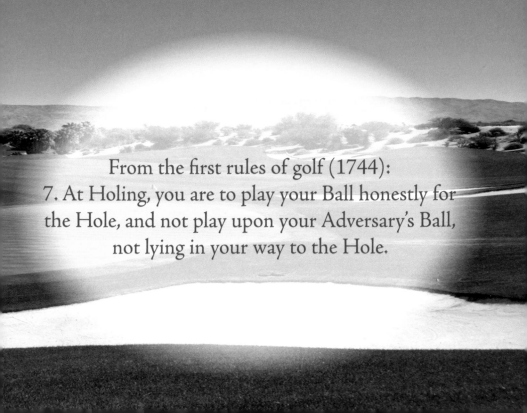

From the first rules of golf (1744):
7. At Holing, you are to play your Ball honestly for the Hole, and not play upon your Adversary's Ball, not lying in your way to the Hole.

From the first rules of golf (1744):
10. If a Ball be stopp'd by any person, Horse, Dog or anything else, the Ball so stopp'd must be played where it lyes.

He who keeps the law is a discerning son.

PROVERBS 28:7 NIV

The first British Open was held in
Prestwick, Scotland, in 1860.

The first U.S. Open Championship was held in Newport, Rhode Island, in 1895.

Five golf clubs—St. Andrews in Yonkers, New York; Shinnecock Hills in Southampton, New York; Newport in Rhode Island; the Country Club in Boston; and the Chicago Golf Club—joined to form the United States Golf Association in 1894.

A grandfather and a great-grandfather
of President George W. Bush each served
as president of the USGA.

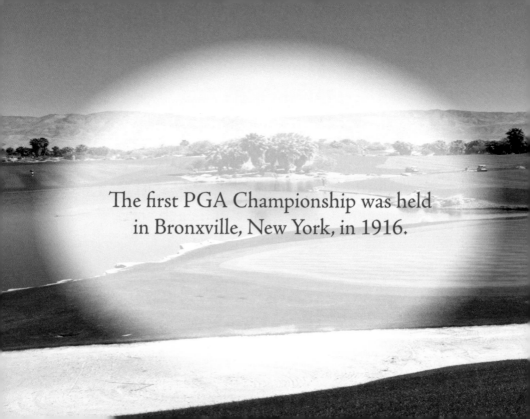

The first PGA Championship was held in Bronxville, New York, in 1916.

The Ladies' Professional Golf Association
was formed in 1948.

"*Where two or three come together in my name, there am I with them.*"

MATTHEW 18:20 NIV

The Personalities
of Golf

"I've got mae God and
mae gowff to see me thro.'"

"OLD TOM" MORRIS,
FOUR-TIME BRITISH OPEN CHAMPION

Notable golfers with appropriate names:
Gary Player (1935–)
Tiger Woods (1975–)
Hubert Green (1946–)
John Ball (1861–1940)

South Korean golfers Mi-Hyun Kim, Gloria Park, Hee Won Han, and Se Ri Pak have been dubbed "the Seoul Sisters."

LPGA Hall of Famer Nancy Lopez
is married to 1986 World Series Most
Valuable Player Ray Knight.

"*The reason the pro tells you to keep your head down is so you can't see him laughing.*"

PHYLLIS DILLER

A cheerful heart is good medicine,
but a crushed spirit dries up the bones.

PROVERBS 17:22 NIV

Golfing legend Bobby Jones lost the 1925 U.S. Open due to a self-imposed penalty.

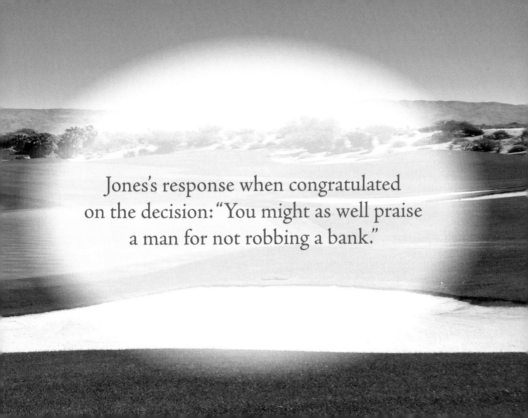

Jones's response when congratulated
on the decision: "You might as well praise
a man for not robbing a bank."

Argentine Robert DiVicenzo lost the 1968 Masters by a single stroke when he carelessly signed an incorrect scorecard; his partner had accidentally marked DiVicenzo for a par 4 instead of the correct birdie 3 on the 17th hole.

DiVicenzo's response during the Masters awards banquet: "What a stupid I am!"

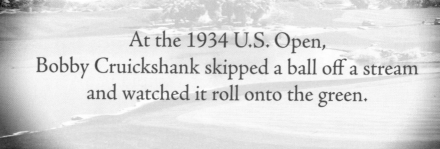

At the 1934 U.S. Open,
Bobby Cruickshank skipped a ball off a stream
and watched it roll onto the green.

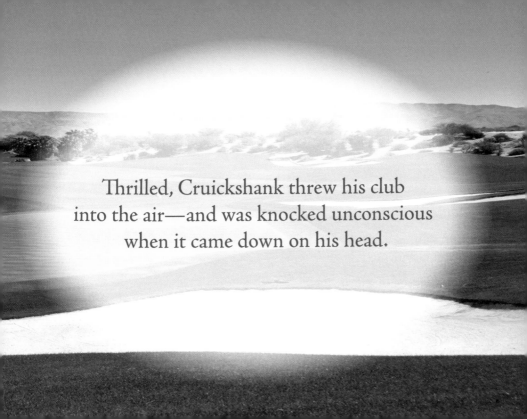

Thrilled, Cruickshank threw his club into the air—and was knocked unconscious when it came down on his head.

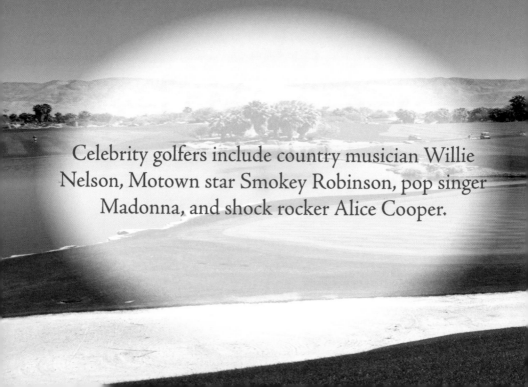

Celebrity golfers include country musician Willie Nelson, Motown star Smokey Robinson, pop singer Madonna, and shock rocker Alice Cooper.

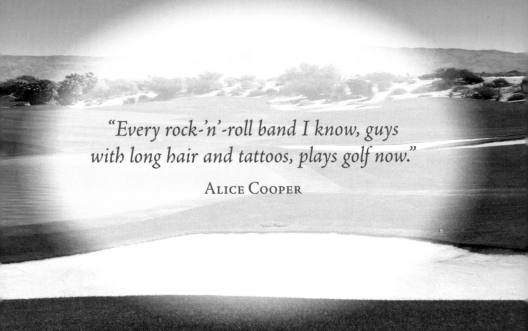

"Every rock-'n'-roll band I know, guys with long hair and tattoos, plays golf now."

ALICE COOPER

"*Come with me by yourselves to a quiet place and get some rest.*"

MARK 6:31 NIV

Golf and Politics

In presidential elections, golfers—such as George H. W. Bush, Bill Clinton, and George W. Bush—generally defeat non-golfers—such as Michael Dukakis, Bob Dole, Al Gore, and John Kerry.

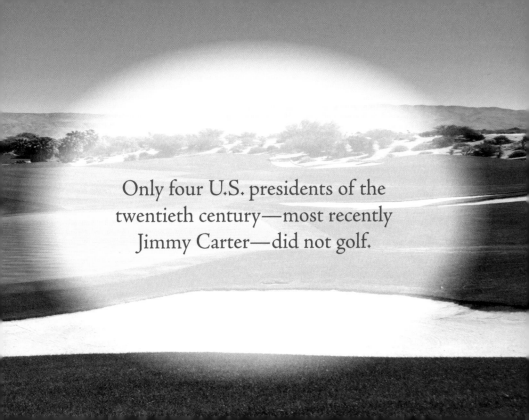

Only four U.S. presidents of the twentieth century—most recently Jimmy Carter—did not golf.

Dwight D. Eisenhower, an avid golfer, had a putting green installed at the White House during his presidency.

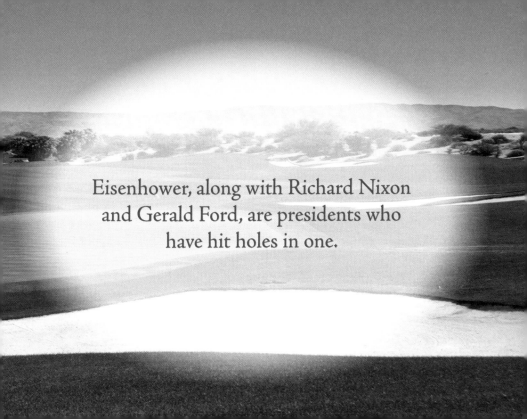

Eisenhower, along with Richard Nixon and Gerald Ford, are presidents who have hit holes in one.

One of the best presidential golfers,
John F. Kennedy, came within six inches
of a hole in one a few months before
his 1960 election victory.

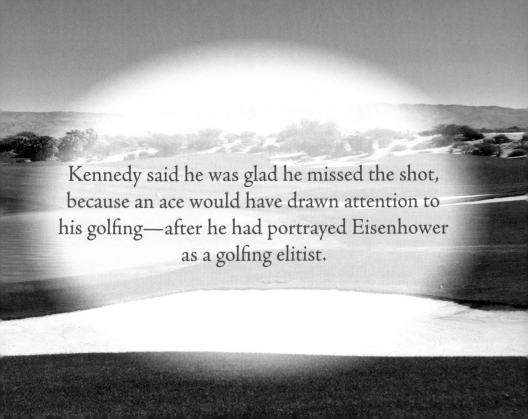

Kennedy said he was glad he missed the shot, because an ace would have drawn attention to his golfing—after he had portrayed Eisenhower as a golfing elitist.

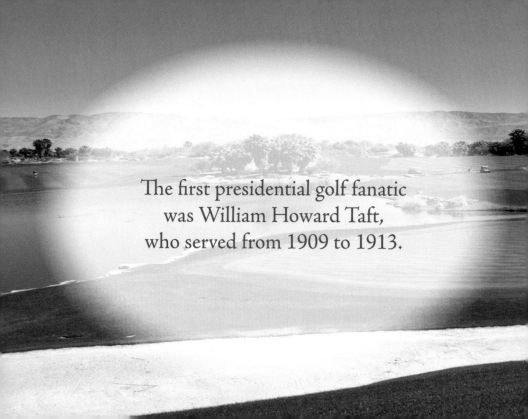

The first presidential golf fanatic
was William Howard Taft,
who served from 1909 to 1913.

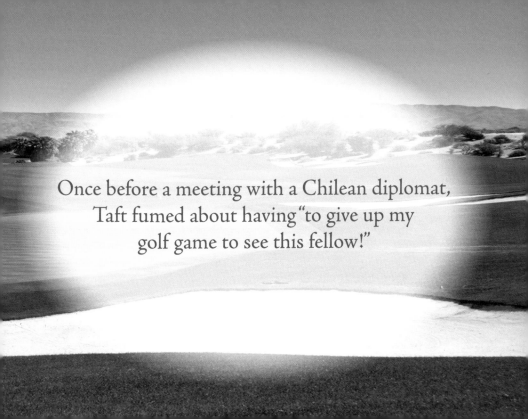

Once before a meeting with a Chilean diplomat, Taft fumed about having "to give up my golf game to see this fellow!"

North Korean dictator Kim Jong-Il has
been praised in his official state media
as "the world's greatest golfer."

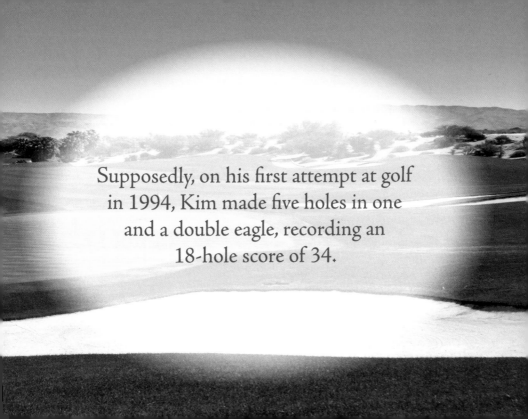

Supposedly, on his first attempt at golf
in 1994, Kim made five holes in one
and a double eagle, recording an
18-hole score of 34.

One lesson you'd better learn if you want to be in politics is that you never get out on a golf course and beat the president.

LYNDON BAINES JOHNSON

Holes in One

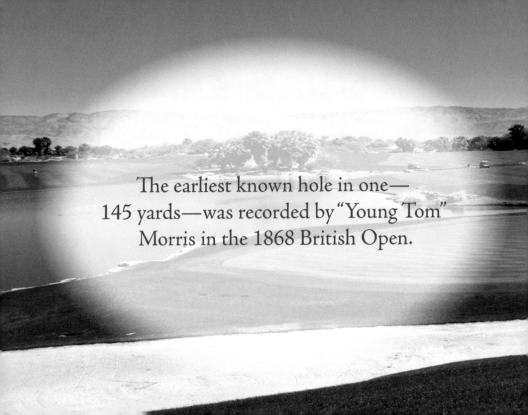

The earliest known hole in one—
145 yards—was recorded by "Young Tom"
Morris in the 1868 British Open.

The longest known hole in one belongs to Robert Mitera, who aced a 444-yard hole in Omaha in October 1965.

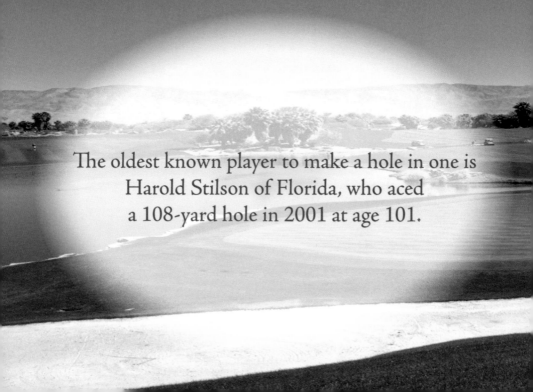

The oldest known player to make a hole in one is
Harold Stilson of Florida, who aced
a 108-yard hole in 2001 at age 101.

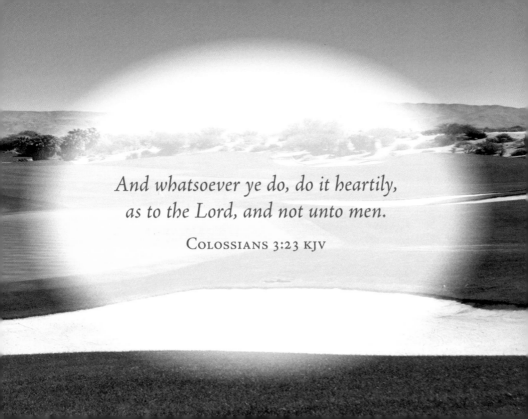

And whatsoever ye do, do it heartily,
as to the Lord, and not unto men.

COLOSSIANS 3:23 KJV

PGA star Tiger Woods sunk his first hole in one when he was six years old.

The LPGA's Michelle Wie recorded her first ace at age twelve.

Golf legends Jack Nicklaus and Arnold Palmer have twenty and eighteen holes in one, respectively.

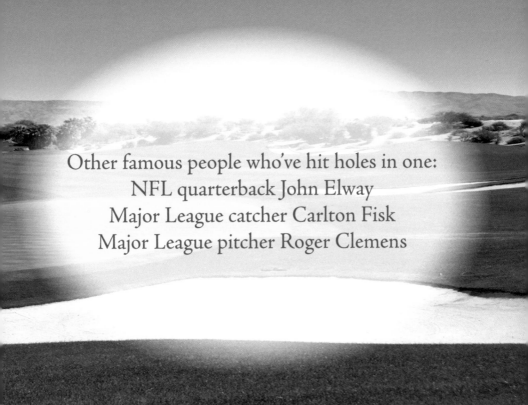

Other famous people who've hit holes in one:
NFL quarterback John Elway
Major League catcher Carlton Fisk
Major League pitcher Roger Clemens

The odds of an amateur acing
a par-3 hole: 12,500 to 1.

Amateur golfer Norman Manley of
Long Beach, California, has nearly
five dozen aces to his credit.

At the 1989 U.S. Open, four players—
Doug Weaver, Mark Wiebe, Jerry Pate,
and Nick Price—aced the 167-yard sixth
hole at the Oak Hill Country Club.

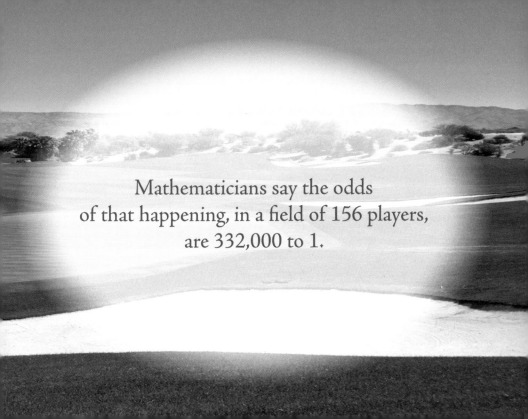

Mathematicians say the odds
of that happening, in a field of 156 players,
are 332,000 to 1.

"With man this is impossible, but not with God;
all things are possible with God."

MARK 10:27 NIV

Milestones and Records, Good and Bad

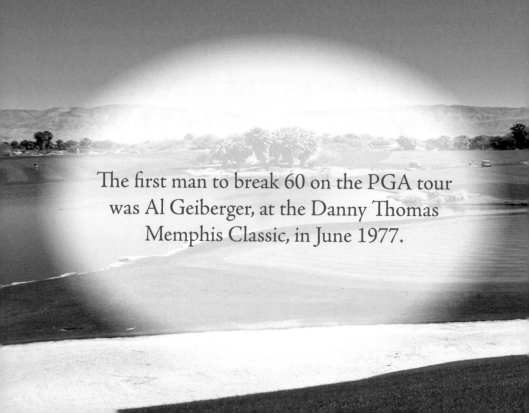

The first man to break 60 on the PGA tour was Al Geiberger, at the Danny Thomas Memphis Classic, in June 1977.

Geiberger shot eleven birdies and an eagle,
putting only twenty-three times, in recording his 59.

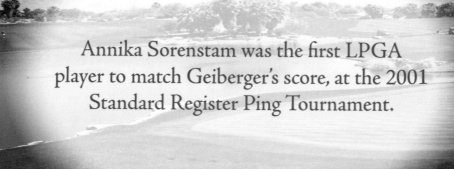

Annika Sorenstam was the first LPGA player to match Geiberger's score, at the 2001 Standard Register Ping Tournament.

Sam Trahan (1979), Mike McGee (1984), Kenny Knox and Andy North (1989), Jim McGovern (1992), and Corey Pavin (2000) have all played an 18-hole PGA event while taking only eighteen putts.

Los Angelino Michael Austin recorded
the game's longest drive on
September 25, 1974: 515 yards.

Playing in the U.S. Seniors' National Open
in Las Vegas, Austin—with a strong tailwind—
overshot the 450-yard fifth hole by 65 yards.

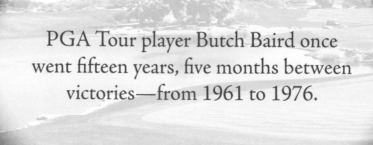

PGA Tour player Butch Baird once
went fifteen years, five months between
victories—from 1961 to 1976.

PGA Tour player Raymond Floyd played almost twenty-nine years between his first and final victories—1963 to 1992.

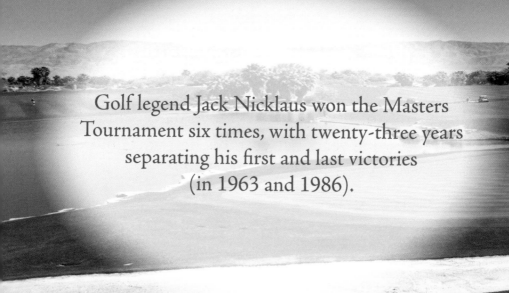

Golf legend Jack Nicklaus won the Masters Tournament six times, with twenty-three years separating his first and last victories (in 1963 and 1986).

Let us not become weary in doing good,
for at the proper time we will reap
a harvest if we do not give up.

GALATIANS 6:9 NIV

In the second round of the 1898 U.S. Open,
J. D. Tucker withdrew after carding a 100.

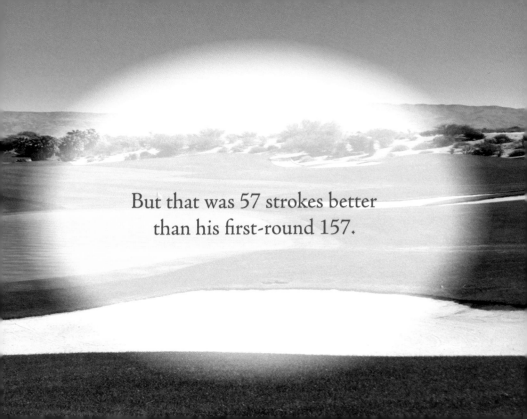

But that was 57 strokes better
than his first-round 157.

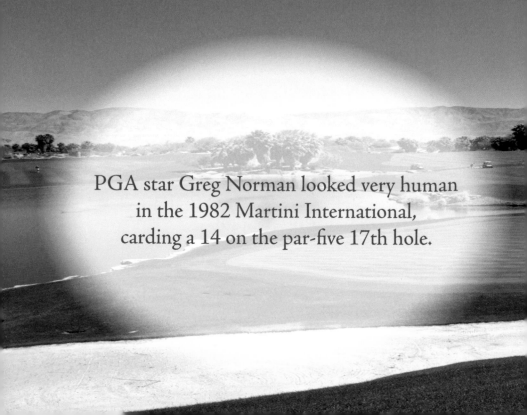

PGA star Greg Norman looked very human
in the 1982 Martini International,
carding a 14 on the par-five 17th hole.

Long-hitting PGA star John Daly, plunking six shots into the water at the 1998 Bay Hill Invitational's par-five 6th hole, recorded an 18.

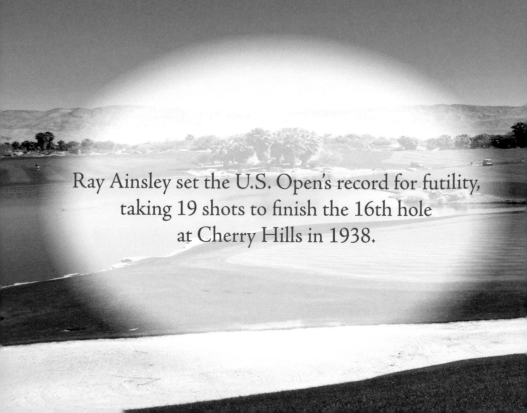

Ray Ainsley set the U.S. Open's record for futility,
taking 19 shots to finish the 16th hole
at Cherry Hills in 1938.

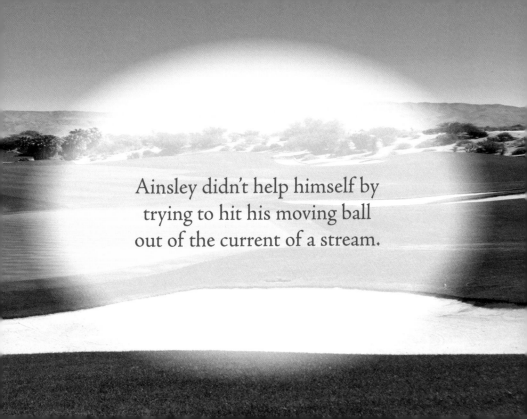

Ainsley didn't help himself by
trying to hit his moving ball
out of the current of a stream.

Therefore do not be foolish,
but understand what the Lord's will is.

EPHESIANS 5:17 NIV

Golf and Money

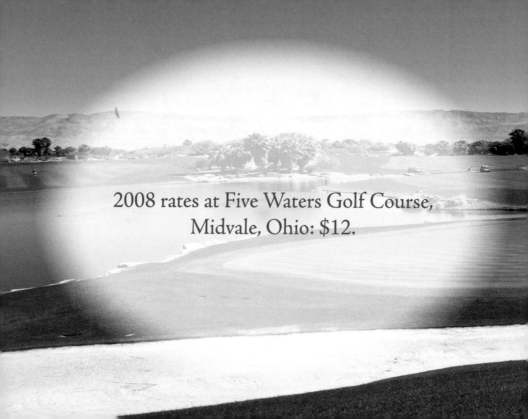

2008 rates at Five Waters Golf Course,
Midvale, Ohio: $12.

2008 rates at Leo Donovan Golf Course,
Peoria, Illinois: $20.

2008 rates at Grande Pines Golf Club,
Orlando, Florida: $103 (average).

2008 rates at the Pebble Beach Golf Links
in California: $495.

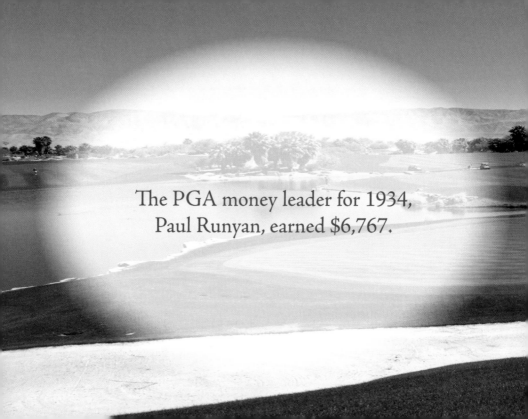

The PGA money leader for 1934,
Paul Runyan, earned $6,767.

The PGA money leader for 2007,
Tiger Woods, earned almost $11 million.

Curtis Strange was the first PGA golfer
to break the million-dollar mark in
single-season earnings, in 1988.

In 2007, Jeff Overton, the 99th-place money earner, took in more than a million dollars.

Command those who are rich in this present world not to be arrogant nor to put their hope in wealth, which is so uncertain, but to put their hope in God, who richly provides us with everything for our enjoyment.

1 Timothy 6:17 niv

Golf in Pop Culture

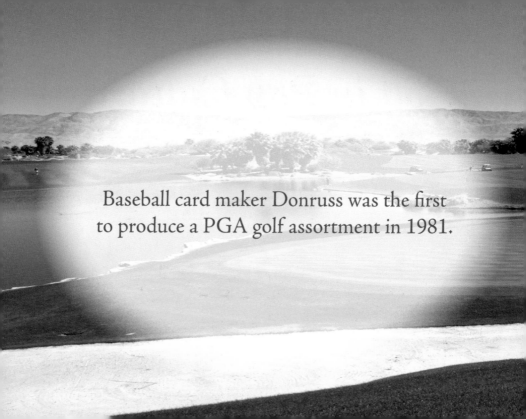

Baseball card maker Donruss was the first to produce a PGA golf assortment in 1981.

In the 1964 movie *Goldfinger*, the evil title character cheats his way through a golf match with Special Agent 007, James Bond.

Well-known actors who've
played in golf movies:
Kevin Costner (*Tin Cup*)
Bill Murray (*Caddyshack*)
Will Smith (*The Legend of Bagger Vance*)

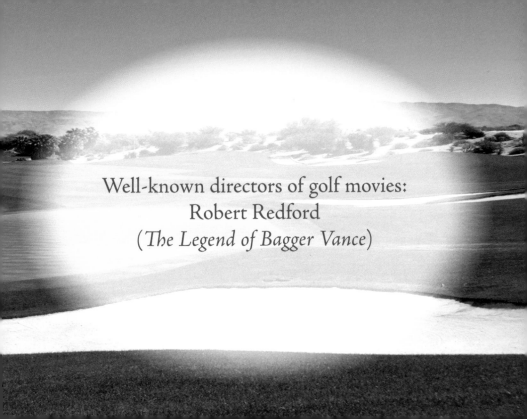

Well-known directors of golf movies:
Robert Redford
(*The Legend of Bagger Vance*)

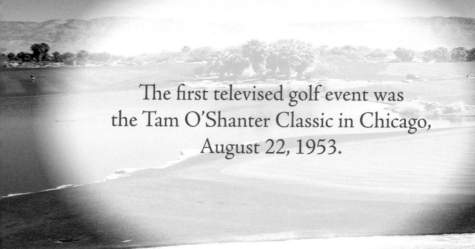

The first televised golf event was
the Tam O'Shanter Classic in Chicago,
August 22, 1953.

Producers were thrilled when competitor Lew Worsham eagled the 18th hole from 115 yards out for a one-stroke victory.

*As we have opportunity, let us do good
to all people, especially to those who
belong to the family of believers.*

GALATIANS 6:10 NIV

Great Quotes from
the Game of Golf

The real way to enjoy golf is to take pleasure not in the score, but in the execution of the strokes.

FROM BOBBY JONES ON GOLF

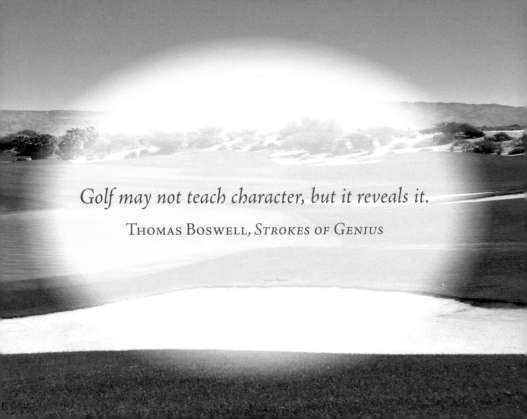

Golf may not teach character, but it reveals it.

THOMAS BOSWELL, STROKES OF GENIUS

In golf, it's never over until the ball is in the hole.

Pate spoke after carding a quadruple-bogey 9 in the 1982 World Series of Golf in Akron, Ohio. He overshot a 50-foot putt for eagle, and a five-footer for birdie, then lipped out the par putt. Frustrated, he made a careless backhand stab for bogey but missed the ball and hit his foot, incurring a two-stroke penalty.

I finally got back on my game.

MARTY FLECKMAN,

1967 U.S. OPEN COMPETITOR

An amateur, the twenty-three-year old Fleckman was challenging for the U.S. Open Championship with rounds of 67, 73, and 69—before shooting a final-round 80 to fall to 18th place.

If you're going to throw a club, it's important to throw it ahead of you, down the fairway, so you don't waste your energy going back to pick it up.

<small>PRO GOLFER TOMMY BOLT</small>

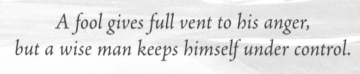

A fool gives full vent to his anger,
but a wise man keeps himself under control.

PROVERBS 29:11 NIV

You can't go into a store and buy a good game of golf.

Golf Miscellany

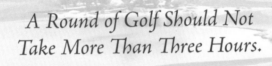

*A Round of Golf Should Not
Take More Than Three Hours.*

SIGN AT AN OLD SCOTTISH GOLF COURSE

The golfer always leaves pets at home.

THE NATIONAL GOLF FOUNDATION,
How to Become a Golfer

A 1998 report to the American Association of Neurological Surgeons described a new medical issue: the "Tiger Woods Syndrome."

According to the report's authors, a rash of "pediatric cranial injuries due to golf club impacts" was due to young boys imitating the up-and-coming PGA star—and accidentally whacking their friends on the head.

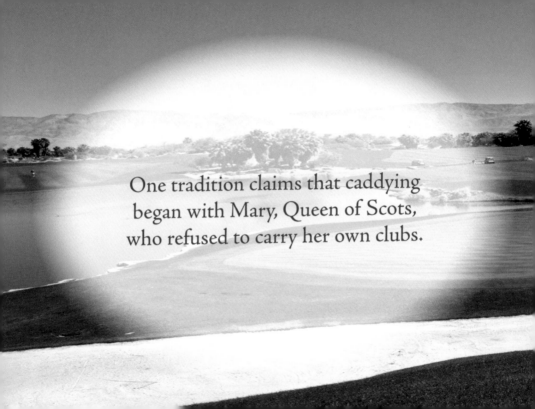

One tradition claims that caddying
began with Mary, Queen of Scots,
who refused to carry her own clubs.

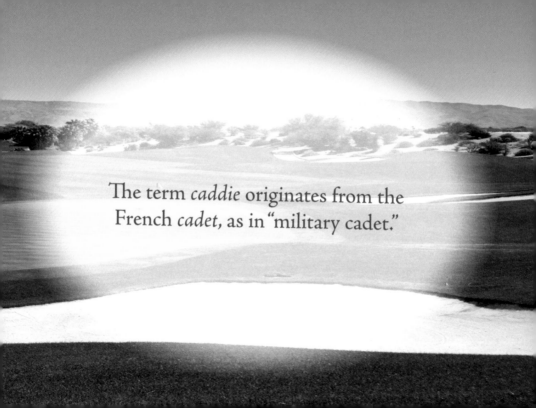

The term *caddie* originates from the French *cadet*, as in "military cadet."

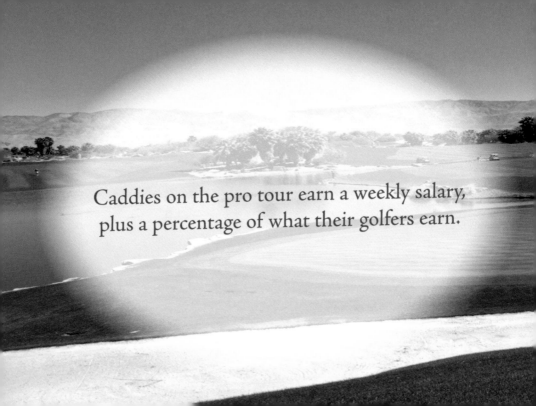

Caddies on the pro tour earn a weekly salary,
plus a percentage of what their golfers earn.

Everyone who competes in the games goes into strict training. They do it to get a crown that will not last; but we do it to get a crown that will last forever.

1 CORINTHIANS 9:25 NIV